# ACTION PHILOSOPHERS!

## A Play by
## Crystal Skillman

### Adapted from the comic book
### by Fred Van Lente and Ryan Dunlavey

D1319821

**chicago** dramaworks

new plays. **chicago style.**

Action Philosophers! (1st ed. 2014)
Copyright © 2014 Crystal Skillman

## Photos from the original production of *Action Philosophers!*

(Left to Right) Kristen Vaughn, Joseph Mathers

(Left to Right) C.L. Weatherstone, Timothy McCown Reynolds, Joseph Mathers. (Top) Neimah Djourabchi

(Left to Right) Joseph Mathers, Kristen Vaughan, Matthew Trumbull

(Left to Right) C.L. Weatherstone, Timothy McCown Reynolds

## Acknowledgements

*Action Philosophers! The Play* was initially produced at The Brick Theater in Brooklyn, New York, on June 23, 2011 in conjunction with the 2011 Comic Book Theater Festival. It was directed by John Hurley; set created by Ben Kato; lighting design by Olivia Harris; costumes by Meryl Pressman & Holly Rihn; props by Gretchen Van Lente; stage management by Veronica Graveline. The cast was as follows:

| | |
|---|---|
| Plato | C.L. Weatherstone |
| Ayn Rand | Kelley Rae O'Donnell |
| Bodhidharma | Neimah Djourabchi |
| Descartes | Ryan Andes |
| Nietzsche | Benjamin Ellis Fine |
| Karl Marx | Joseph Mathers |

*Action Philosophers! The Play* was produced by Impetuous Theater Group at The Brick Theater in Brooklyn, New York, on October 6, 2011. It was directed by John Hurley; lighting & set design by Olivia Harris; costumes by Meryl Pressman & Holly Rihn; props by Gretchen Van Lente; stage management by Audrey Marshall. The cast was as follows:

| | |
|---|---|
| Plato | C.L. Weatherstone |
| Ayn Rand | Kristen Vaughan |
| Bodhidharma | Neimah Djourabchi |
| Descartes | Matthew Trumbull |
| Nietzsche | Timothy McCown Reynolds |
| Karl Marx | Joseph Mathers |

**All productions of this Play are required to include the following credit on the title page of the program:**
The world premiere of *Action Philosophers!* was presented by The Brick Theater in conjunction with the 2011 Comic Book Theater Festival.

*Action Philosophers! The Play* is dedicated to Roger Nasser for insisting that Fred and I finally work together, which set me on the insane mission of adapting my favorite 320 page graphic novel, written by my hubby and drawn by one of my best friends, into a sixty minute play; and to our fearless director John Hurley and our two insanely talented original NYC casts; to the Skillman and Van Lente family for always supporting our dreams - on the page, and now together, on the stage. And most of all to you for reading and joining the insanity! Enjoy!

### Time & Place:
Now. Presenting these stories to you live in your local theatre!

### Note about Staging:
An imaginative, low-budget, playful barebones approach fits the tone of this comedy. The more the audience sees of the "show underneath" such as actors changing quickly, grabbing new props, the more fun it will be. As you'll notice, each story embraces a different genre (Kung Fu for Bodhidhamra, etc.) so embracing that as well is half the fun. If a projection screen is available, the two panels from the comic indicated in the script have permission to be projected, as can the titles of the philosophers if desired between the scenes. Please note those two panels should be credited to artist Ryan Dunlavey. For more information about the original book please visit the Evil Twin Comics site: **http://www.eviltwincomics.com/ap.html**.

### Note about Casting:
This six person ensemble can double as nerds, monks, capitalist pigs, etc. – or the show can easily expand to more, based on desired cast size.

# Action Philosophers!
## by Crystal Skillman
### Adapted from the comic book
### by Fred Van Lente and Ryan Dunlavey

The Action Philosophers!
*In order of appearance*

Plato!

Ayn Rand!

Bodhidharma!

Descartes!

Nietzsche!

Karl Marx!

## OPENING: MEET THE PHILOSOPHERS!

*Fun, action-packed music plays.*

ANNOUNCER
HEY KIDS! Be the first kid on your block to answer these
questions: Who am I? What is the meaning of life? Why
does this pimple on my ass hurt? Do it by collecting them
all: the ACTION PHILOSOPHERS!

*Rock/wrestler type music plays as Plato enters
dramatically through the audience, sporting a toga,
wrestling mask and beard.*

Born ARISTOCLES on the island of Aegina in 428 B.C.,
here's our first Action Philosophers bad boy! The word that
means "broad" or "flat" in Greek was the stage name of
this pro wrestler...PLATO!

PLATO
What hidden truth lies beyond everyday reality?

*Plato takes his place on stage and poses.*

ANNOUNCER
Comes with the following accessories: luchadore mask
and socratic dialogues! Be careful! These are choking
hazards!

*Indian/Kung Fu music plays as Bodhidharma enters.*

A.D. 520. This GRANDMASTER OF KUNG FU –– rocks the
Shaolin Temple atop Sho-shih mountain in rural china.
BODHIDHARMA!

BODHIDHARMA
How does one achieve enlightenment?

ANNOUNCER
With his Koan Kung Fu grip! What is the sound of one hand kicking your ass?!

*Bodhidharma takes his place. Dramatic German operatic war music plays as Marx enters in a Rambo get up.*

This student of Hegel's rejected his idealistic dialectic for a materially determined theory of history but hungered to change the world, not merely interpret it: KARL MARX!

MARX
What is the only way to achieve a just society?

ANNOUNCER
Cut down the enemies of the proletariat with his revolutionary weapons set! Be careful! These are also choking hazards!

*Marx is now in place on stage. Russian music plays as Rand enters.*

This twenty-one-year-old Soviet émigré Alyssa Rosenbaum in 1926 arrives in Los Angeles with stars in her eyes from Leningrad –

RAND
Formerly St. Petersburg.

ANNOUNCER
– to fulfill her lifelong dream of becoming a screenwriter. Don't be conservative with your applause for...AYN RAND!

RAND
What is the only way to achieve a just society?

MARX
I just said that!

*Rand sticks out her tongue at him as she hits her mark.*

ANNOUNCER
Ayn's objectivist eye lights up, exposing the falsehood of metaphysical bullshit and mysticism! Pretty!

*Nietzsche enters, sporting a suit, big black glasses, and a barber's moustache (of course).*

ANNOUNCER
Next: 1844 born to a long line of preachers near modern day Leipzig, Germany, this superman retires from the philology department of the university of Basel Switzerland but develops his critique of western society! Comes with mustache, cape ... and syphilis! Mmmmm! SYPHILIS!! Friedrich "The Übermensch" Nietzsche!

*He rips open his shirt -- a la Superman - exposing his Ubermensch Symbol.*

NIETZSCHE
History is moving in one direction -- but why? And to whose benefit?

*He "flies" off -- which most likely means jumping off a block dramatically.*

ANNOUNCER
And...last but not least: the father of modern philosophy
who in 1619 hit upon his revolutionary theory holed up in
a cabin in winter while serving in the thirty years war. Rene
- Descartes? Baby?  Yoo hoo?

*Beat. No one enters.*

MARX
Descartes - what are you doing?

NIETZSCHE
Where the hell are you?

DESCARTES (OFF)
I'm here.

PLATO
Come out here then!

BODHIDHAMRA
Hit your mark. We all did.

RAND
The show must go on!

DESCARTES (OFF)
I know! I'm excited to do my bit but well...um-

MARX
WHAT?!

DESCARTES (OFF)
We are all here to demonstrate the foundations of our
philosophy, oui?

NIETZSCHE
No shit.

DESCARTES (OFF)
B-but... central to my method is hyperbolic doubt. I critique everything I used to think I know. I reject anything I cannot prove by ironclad logic.

RAND
Okay. And so?

DESCARTES (OFF)
Well... as a result of all this doubting ... I doubt whether or not I actually exist!

MARX
Oh, you've gotta be shitting me.

BODHIDHARMA
This is crazy.

PLATO
Wait! Plato can demonstrate Plato exists.

NIETZSCHE
How?

PLATO
Because Plato SMASH!

*Plato does a huge wrester jump move on Nietzsche... which transitions seamlessly into our first story!*

## MEET ACTION PHILOSOPHER # 1: PLATO!

*Wresting music up. Plato struts around excited. Rand "pins" him as the Ref judges.*

REF
Plato. You might be the two-time champ of the Isthmian Games -- but the Olympics? Forget it.

*He forcefully thrusts a paper bag which says "Plato's Stuff" into Plato's hands.*

PS.

*Plato turns back, Ref whispers.*

You suck.

PLATO
Plato's mighty heart breaking...what big man with big heart does that means anything in this cruel world?

*Something like Kenny Rogers "Just Dropped In" plays as Socrates -- a Big Know It All Cool Lebowski-like dude -- walks in.*

SOCRATES
No man is as wise as Socrates, and that is me!! I got the all the answers cuz I got me some philosophy. You can too if you join my group.

PLATO
Really?

SOCRATES
We love outcasts. We're totally about sticking it to the man, man. Watch this! *(calling for him)* Oh Mr. Authority Priest Dude!

*Priest appears.*

PRIEST
What now Socrates?

SOCRATES
Truth totally can't be found in religion!

PRIEST
So if religion is B.S., then you tell me: what is Truth?

SOCRATES
I do not know.

PRIEST
What? Then how can you be wiser than everybody else?

SOCRATES
Because I KNOW that I do not know.

PRIEST
By Zeus, you're a pain in the ass.

*Priest storms off.*

PLATO
Wow. That's awesome. You're awesome!

SOCRATES
I know, dude. Say, if you like my dialectic critiques, check out my students!

*Punk appears and confronts Priest.*

PRIEST
This guy's crazy! If you boys are searching for truth, you should look to Zeus!

PUNK
Are Zeus's actions arbitrary, or is he guided by truth too?

PRIEST
Of course Zeus is guided by Truth!

PUNK
Well, in that case, I should just look for Truth...

*Punk turns and gives Priest the finger.*

...for a wise man would not need Zeus!

*Priest fumes as Punk student and Socrates laugh.*

PLATO
Awesome! Sign me up!

PRIEST
"Dialect THIS mofo!"

*Priest blows a whistle.*

Athenian Riot Cop One! Athenian Riot Cop two! Get him!

*Athenian Riot Cops beat up the Punk. Priest points to Socrates.*

PRIEST
And get them too!

*Socrates and Plato run in place as the cops pursue, but Socrates falls behind.*

SOCRATES
Oh no. Flip flops failing! Run fella! Don't forget what I taught ya –ahhhh!

*Plato runs off, escaping. He quickly re-enters.*

PLATO
Oh! Where am I?

*Godfather theme plays. He realizes:*

PLATO
Oh Sicily! Plato safe. And lonely.

NERDS (OFF)
ALL IS NUMBER! ALL IS NUMBER!

*Three math nerds in white robes pop up and down hiding in various places, looking at Plato curiously.*

PLATO
Ugh. Math Hippies!

*The head nerd approaches.*

HEAD NERD
Pythagoreans if you please! Pythagoras– of triangle theorem fame–founded us! Behold!

NERD TWO
We comprehend the nature of the cosmos through numbers!

NERD THREE
To purify our minds for mystic calculations, we have taken
a vow of secrecy!

HEAD NERD
Wear only white!

NERD TWO
And have sworn off sexual intercourse.

NERD THREE
Sorry ladies. Wanna hang out?

PLATO
Well ok – I guess I have enough bean salad to share for
lunch.

*He holds out his "Plato's Stuff" bag full of beans, and the
Nerds run away.*

HEAD NERD
AHHHH!

NERD TWO
A bean!

NERD THREE
Don't touch it! Beans are prohibited.

HEAD NERD
So we have some weird rules okay? But it's all for one
goal: so we can focus on our material universe which is
the imperfect expression of a higher, abstract universe...a
perfect and harmonious realm of number.

*It's like in "Simpsons language" when Homer is being
shown "the land of chocolate". Happy music plays and the
Nerds take out happy colorful numbers that dance by him.*

PLATO
Ohhh realm of numbers - WAIT!

*He pushes math nerds/numbers away with his realization.*

Plato knows he know what Socrates knew he did <u>not</u>
know! Real truth is abstract, and, like numbers,
unchanging...eternal! Existence emanates from a higher
essence: The Realm of Forms!

*Projector light comes on or light from a flashlight comes
up on a screen. As Plato philosophizes, the math nerds
discover they can project their own shadows which starts
out innocent but grows more mocking or graphic.*

Imagine the condition of men as living in a sort of
underground cavern. Here men can only see in front of
them. Higher up, and some distance behind them, is the
light of a burning fire. Before the fire is a parapet.
Behind the parapet imagine there are men carrying all
kinds of objects – including figures of men and animals
which project above the parapet. In all ways, men would
consider reality to be nothing else than the shadows of
those artificial objects! *(refers to his own shadow)* But that
isn't enough! We must look beyond these shadows of our
perceived reality –

*Actors are making fun of Plato, making him upset.*

-- and uncover the forms that project them! PLATO
SMASH!! PLATO --

*An actor trumpets and hands him a scroll.*

For me? I got a job! I'm invited to be the Court Philosopher to –

*Dionysius appears stuffing his face.*

Dionysius. King of Syracuse! (Hope I don't fuck it up.)

*Dionysius keeps stuffing his face, getting grosser and grosser.*

This job is great! Great. People are starting to really listen to me, read my books. You know The Republic? Uh-huh. Well - fun! This is fun. No more wrestling for me. Nope. Just serving pompous people like you and- good God lord must you be so...carnal?

DIONYSIUS
You speak like a geriatric fool!

PLATO
And you speak like a tyrant!

*Plato is shackled and hauled away by Slave Driver.*

PLATO
*Sigh!* Plato have this PROBLEM with AUTHORITY...

SLAVE DRIVER
Got yer Action Philosopher slave for sale here. Action Philosopher slave for sale! Don't be cheap! We got change for a dollar!

PLATO (*Comically sobbing*)
Plato do ANYTHING, just don't want to get REAL JOB!!
HELP!!

*Head Nerd enters, pays for Plato.*

HEAD NERD
Here. We sold our protractor collection to help you.

PLATO
Yes! Saved by Philosophy!

*Slave Driver frees Plato.*

WAIT!

*Plato excitedly spreads his arms again knocking the Head Nerd over.*

What if we had a place – where like-minded people can gather. Get rid of your mondo-bizzaro bean phobias...but keep it about numbers, keep Socrates' (may he rest in hemlock peace) knee-jerk critiquing, the Theory of Forms as an operating VALUE SYSTEM, I'll call it – AKADEMOS! Or-

*College kids pop up drinking and partying and running around "Animal House style" shouting:*

COLLEGE KIDS
COLLEGE!

*Something like Wooly Bully plays as Plato goes around trying to impress his students at the party.*

PLATO
Yes! Now I have job and can write all I want! I'll use what my first teacher Socrates taught me...his teachings will be resurrected!

*Socrates enters Zombie style, drunk at the party.*

SOCRATES
BRAINS!! Must...use...BRAINS!!

PLATO
I'll write Socrates in all my papers. The Apology.

SOCRATES *(Hitting on a girl)*
Since I do not know what comes after death, why should I fear it?

PLATO
And in the Republic I use his same absolutes to propose the perfect society!

SOCRATES *(Hitting on another girl)*
Give me your babies! The government will raise them! Muwhwhahahahah.

*He passes out while Plato gets more and more drunk.*

PLATO
Yes! In my perfect republic world - you!

*He picks out different students, giving them orders.*

You flunk gym and become a farmer! You – you flunk math, you go in the military! And if you're good at gym and math you get to study...wait for it. PHILOSOPHY!!

PLATO (CONT.)
And one of the 35 would be chosen to be the Philosopher King who would rule over all. We philosopher-rulers would sleep together, work together, sleep together. Plato would force human society to adhere to the impossible, abstract standard of the Realm of Forms! I would reach – the ULTIMATE PHILOSOPHER FANTASY! My ideas would last for all time (and we'd sleep together).

*Smart, classical music plays. A pompous professor enters and addresses the audience as his classroom.*

PROFESSOR
Attention class!

PLATO
So all you Brooklyn College students and Yale grads out there *(pointing at an audience member)* - Sarah Lawrence. If you think your professors are a little dictatorial –

PROFESSOR
Students! Look to your right. And left. Only one of you will pass the most important college class I'm teaching this semester -

*Hits remote. The Projection below (from comic) comes up:*

*Professor dramatically exclaims as he uses a laser pointer to demonstrate.*

PROFESSOR (CONT.)
The subliminal Reinscribement of Phallo-Centril Specialist Hegemony in 1980s Videogames is most apparent in the psychic sexual tropes of "Burger Time!"

*Plato, now drunk, follows the laser pointer as Professor messes with him. The laser hits the wall, which Plato follows, smashing into the wall.*

PROFESSOR
Ah Realm of Forms...!

*Plato wises up, grabs the chair, and goes after him wrestler-style.*

PLATO
PLATO SMASH!

*Plato chases Professor off.*

## OBJECTIVELY SPEAKING, ACTION PHILOSOPHER #2: AYN RAND!

*Russian music creeps in. As she speaks, Rand steps into the projection of the movie* King of Kings.

RAND
The task of man's consciousness is to percieve reality -- not to create or invent it! My father, a bourgeois pharmacist, was ruined by the Communist revolution in Russia when his business was nationalized. My only place to escape was in the fantasy world of the movies. On the silver screen I could see America -- where individual achievement was rewarded, not confiscated! So I came here -- to California! HOLLYWOOD!

*Music changes to something Hollywood and fun.*

Where I know -- Boys --

*Boys enter and lift her up Marilyn Monroe/"Moulin Rouge" style.*

-- I could be more than accepted. I could be...a star!

*They drop her off at DeMille Studios. She waves them off.*

RAND
Excuse  - Mr. DeMille here? Me writes movies, you like hire me, no?

DEMILLE
A little creaky with the English there aren't you ruskie --

RAND
But me have - heart.

*She turns around, back to audience, rips open her shirt and flashes her "heart" to Mr. DeMille. She might have to do this a few times. He doesn't bat an eyelash.*

DEMILLE
Welcome to the movies, kid. You're hired.

RAND
But me want to write.

DEMILLE
But if you act - you don't have to say a thing! Who cares about your awful English or that crazy accent. It's silent. Just remember your godly motivation when you meet the *King of Kings*!

RAND
Jesus is oppressor.

DEMILLE
Aw. You tasty Russian treat. Caviar! That's what I'll call ya.

*Rand bumps into Frank who is playing Jesus.*

FRANK
Hey! Look where you're going - you almost made me miss the crucifixion!

RAND
Me sorry. I go. You make playtime prayer.

FRANK
I think my prayers have already been answered.

*Rand laughs loudly, then smiles.*

FRANK (CONT.)
I'm Frank. And who are you?

*She kisses him. Whenever she kisses anyone, it's rough.
She is definitely in charge.*

RAND
Your wife.

*Happy domestic 50's music plays.*

FRANK
Yes! Married life has always been my dream! White picket
fence! Coffee in the morning, clean house...but we've
been married for like, years now, and the reality is you
haven't done the dishes or taken out the garbage or had
any kids - WHY?

*Rand turns, proudly holds book* We The Living *– which
also says "AYN RAND" on the cover.*

RAND
Because I'm a writer!

FRANK
Who's -- *(mispronounces)* "Ayn" ...?

RAND *(Correcting him)*
AYN. Alyssa Rosenbaum is no more! So KGB can never
touch my family. I'm Ayn Rand now. And all will love my
book. Perfect for the great depression! It's all anti-
communist -- can't wait to share about the glory of
capitalism with all our Hollywood friends.

FRANK
Honey, have you been on the red carpet lately?

*Clueless Movie Star gives acceptance speech as Rand fumes.*

MOVIE STAR
Like Comrade Stalin has created a utopia for the workingman in Russia--we like here in America could totally learn from him!

RAND
Pampered, pompous FOOLS! They're just spouting the fantasies they <u>want</u> to believe!

*DeMille bugs her.*

DEMILLE
Caviar honey - you're late! Aren't you supposed to be doing research on that new project - the whose-he-what's-it big tall thing--

RAND
Skyscraper.

DEMILLE
That's what I said. Writing crazy books about crazy philosophy will never make you happy! All there is...is lights! Camera! Action!

*DeMille walks away.*

RAND
Philosophy isn't crazy! Mine will be the greatest in the world, once I find it.

*Architects sexily strut in -- flex muscles as they lift T-squares and lay out rulers.*

RAND
So architects - making something out of nothing.
Rebuilding. How do you do it?

ARCHITECT ONE
It takes a long time. It's hard.

ARCHITECT TWO
But man can conquer nature!

ARCHITECT ONE
When it's all about the foundation.

*Rand grabs him excitedly. Kisses!*

RAND
It's a VALUE SYSTEM! A equals A. Objectivist philosophy is the law of identity!

*She gets more and more excited – which might mean physically abusing the men on every capitalized moment.*

Nature has bestowed on EVERY organism but MAN inborn abilities to survive in its environment! Man does not even have the INSTINCTS beasts have to INNATELY understand the world around them! Innately!  The ONLY tools man can use to APPREHEND and CONQUER the world around him are the JUDGMENTAL powers of his REASON! To reject REASON is to DENY man his most BASIC means of SURVIVAL! To be anti-MIND is to be anti-LIFE!

*An actor throws her a pill bottle which she catches.*

Oh! Pills. Taking these will help me stay up and finish my book.

*She downs the pills and starts coming up with THE FOUNTAINHEAD. As she does one of the architects becomes Howard. Actors hold up a cliff painted on a sheet or he stands behind something.*

RAND (CONT.)
"Howard Roark laughed...

*He laughs.*

...stood naked at the edge of cliff!

*Roark whips off shirt, throws up pants, and finally underwear, disguised only by his "cliff." Rand approaches.*

RAND
My Howard - thwarted by "the hostility of second-hand souls" who try to force us to conform and compromise us, but we won't, will we...?

HOWARD
I give you...my ego and my naked need.

*Sexy! They go to kiss. Frank enters with a newspaper that reads:*

FRANK
*Fountainhead!* It's a best seller!

HOWARD
Good job Ain!

*Howard exits.*

RAND *(Corrects him)*
Ayn! But some of these reviews. Not positive. Why?

FRANK
I don't know honey, but I was thinking chicken tonight, what do you think?

RAND
Why won't they all love my ideas? Why would anyone want to destroy it? Because they're looters!

FRANK
Chicken it is.

*Frank happily leaves.*

RAND
It will all be in my next book how the looters have been trying to get people to sacrifice themselves for "society's" good – like your family!

*As Rand describes these roles, one actor plays them, throwing on different costume pieces quickly.*

JEWISH MOTHER
Become an artist? You want to kill your mother, Herschel?! No, you'll become a doctor. It's for the good of the family!

RAND
Your government!

S.S. COMMANDANT
Shove them in the ovens like you were told, Corporal Schmidt! It is for the good of the white race!

RAND
What they do to your own father! Dad!

*Rand's Dad enters. Soviet Commisar wags finger at him. This bit could also be played by the same actor switching back and forth.*

COMMISSAR
You will turn all the profits of your pharmacy over to the state, Comrade Rosenbaum! It is for the good of the proletariat!

*Dad sadly walks off, and Rand reaches out to him.*

RAND
Dad! The Looters ruined him!

*Holy music. Jesus on the cross rises up. If doubling, it works well to have Jesus played by the actor playing Frank.*

The most naked evocation of Looter "values"- Christianity! Their cross represents the torture and murder of a superior being for the sins of His inferiors! Looters are from man's tribal past. Civilization is the process of setting man free from men!

JESUS
Hey.... You've got a point... I'm the SON of GOD, for my sakes! What the heck am I doin'? I'm goin' to Disneyland!

*Jesus and the cross bounce away to Mickey Mouse theme song.*

Thanks Ayn! *(Pronounced wrong)*

RAND
Ayn! And I'm going to my new book signing. *Atlas Shrugged* author here! Hello?

*Right Wing and Hippie run on.*

RIGHT WING
She rejects religion! She's a leftist nut job!

HIPPIE
All she loves is money! She's a right-wing fascist!

*They exit.*

RAND
Ok, now I'm like seriously really depressed.

*Pills are thrown to her again, and she takes more.*
*Nathaniel enters and approaches. If doubling, it works*
*well to have Nathaniel played by the pompous Professor*
*in Plato's scene.*

NATHANIEL
Uh ... Ayn? *(finally says her name right!)* It's -- Nathaniel. I
love your books, man. I'm doing psychiatry now and using
Objectivism in my practice. People love it. Your ideas. After
all, self-esteem is the consequence -

RAND
-of a mind fully committed to reason!

NATHANIEL
My wife Barbara and I formed a school ... National
Branden Institute - N.B.I. Totally inspired by your
teachings. Devoted to you...

RAND
You.

NATHANIEL
Yes?

RAND
You could be my spokesperson. My intellectual heir. Our romance ....

NATHANIEL
Yes...?

RAND
Will be all...very...logical.

*They kiss. Frank enters.*

FRANK
Hi Honey, it's me Frank. Say - who's that fella in the living room you're making out with?

*As Rand talks to him, a Bimbo enters and seduces Nathaniel. He runs to her and they make out.*

RAND
Frank - you must recognize the rationality of what Nate and I feel for each other...yes! Self-control is the name of the game and –

FRANK
So you're leaving me for that guy making out with that bimbo?

*Rand sees Nate making out with bimbo. She goes ape-shit crazy.*

RAND
WHAT THE HELL ARE YOU DOING? You DARE reject me--
ME-- for--for a mental INFERIOR?!

*SLAP!! Ayn slaps Nathaniel—savagely and repeatedly!*

I'll DESTROY you as I CREATED you! I don't even care what
it does to ME! You'll have NOTHING-- just as you STARTED,
just as you came to me, just as you would have remained
WITHOUT me! If you have an ounce of morality left in you,
an OUNCE of psychological health—you'll be impotent for
the next twenty years! Shut it down.  Shut it all down.

*She starts to go. DeMille enters.*

DEMILLE
It's a downer way to end a picture honey!  Star gives up
her dreams. Objectivism's main school will cease to exist.
Your ideas lost!

RAND
Everyone –the world- has been all this time indifferent to
my ideas. Let them.

DEMILLE
Sounds like a self-fulfilling prophecy, baby!

*Rand turns with a "Gone with the Wind" type of passion.*

RAND
I still have – my reason!

*Rand makes her grand Hollywood exit.*

## HEY KIDS! MEET ACTION PHILOSOPHER #3: BODHIDHARMA!

*Sound of Gong! Monks scurry on.*

MONK ONE
Did you hear? BODHIDHARMA has arrived in China! At our Shao-shih mountain!

*Unseen by Monks, Bodhidarma is walking up behind them as his Indian theme music plays softly.*

MONK TWO
I hear after being the famed patriarch of the Dhyana School of Buddhism he decided to become a poor missionary, preaching in foreign lands, when his own teacher died!

MONK THREE
I hear he was born to vast wealth in southern India, but he gave it all up to follow the path of the Enlightened One!

MONK ONE
I hear he walked here all the way from India!

*Bodhidarma reveals he is right behind the monks!*

MONKS
Ah!

*Sound of Gong!*

MONKS
EMPEROR WU!

*Wu stiffly and pompously walks on. They bow down to the Emperor.*

EMPEROR WU
I have built many temples and monasteries. I - and all my three monks - have copied the sacred books of the Buddha. Now WHAT is my merit stranger?

BODHIDHARMA
None WHATSOEVER, your Majesty!

*Gasp!*

EMPEROR WU
What are you saying boy?

BODHIDHARMA
In Buddhism, only enlightenment—the annihilation of the self—can liberate a person's consciousness to experience unmediated, objective reality.

EMPEROR WU
I know! And enlightenment can only be achieved through years and years and years and years and years and years of studying scripture.

BODHIDHARMA
I don't buy that. The Buddha did not have his own teachings. Yet He became enlightened. What do the rest of us need it for? I say you see Buddha on the street–

*Budda enters and waves.*

Kill him!

*Bodhidharma does Kung Fu kick and Buddha goes flying. Monks look at him, saying things like "oh no you didn't" and/or "that is so hot."*

EMPEROR WU
Such heresy could not be allowed inside the hallowed halls of Shaolin Temple!

*...which, with the actor's insanely bad accent, sounds more like:*

BODHIDHARMA
Shirley Temple...?

*This can go on for a bit with Wu trying to get it right until:*

EMPEROR WU
I don't like you! Shut the gates!

*He runs back to the curtain.*

Shut the gates!

*He's gone. Monks turn their backs becoming "human doors."*

MONKS
SLAM!

*Bodhidarma sits in lotus position outside Monk wall.*

MONK ONE
He's still waiting there! In the wind.

*The monks blow on him and fan him.*

MONK TWO
In the rain!

*Sprays him with water.*

MONK THREE
In the snow!

*Throws snow at him. Bodhidharma remains in perfect position!*

MONK ONE
It's been nine years!

MONK TWO
Maybe he really DOES have something to show us!

MONK ONE
Let's let him in!

MONK THREE
I don't know. That makes me afraid and worried. And afraid.

BODHIDHARMA
Why? What do you fear?

MONK THREE *(Actor can feel free to riff or add)*
Doors. Cats. Carpal Tunnel Syndrome. Traffic. Beef Jerky. Accurate expiration dates. Death. Oh god - please pacify my mind!

BODHIDHARMA
SHOW ME this mind, so that I may pacify it.

MONK THREE
Huh? But I can't show you my mind!

BODHIDHARMA
Well, then...I have pacified it!

MONK ONE
How did you do that?!

BODHIDHARMA
Koans! It is what I teach in my Dhayma school.

MONK TWO
Where is it?

BODHIDHARMA
I'm starting it here right now!

MONKS
Yay!

*They jump for joy.*

BODHIDHARMA
Pay attention!

*He starts doing some Kung Fu moves. They follow.*

All that is comes from the mind; it is based on the mind; it is fashioned by the mind.

*A Skater Kid, hunched over listening to music, enters.*

To be at peace with the world, first you have to be at peace with yourself—and that is easier said than done!

SKATER KID
Yeah, right! I'M keepin' it REAL! Ahhhh!

*Bodhidharama grabs him by the neck in a move á la Star Trek, paralyzing him for a moment. Bodhidhamra "defines" Skater Kid to audience.*

BODHIDHARMA
White. Straight. Male. American. Erie, Pennsylvania. Upper middle class. Divorced parents, lives with daddy.

SKATER KID
Hey - it's only temporary!

BODHIDHARMA
Oh? How can you be so sure "you are keeping it real," when the "REAL" you keep is so specific to you alone? You perceive what is real only as it is strained through your consciousness...but your consciousness is biased toward your own sense of identity, or self!

SKATER KID
It's true.

*Skater kid straightens up. Now enlightened, he hugs Bodhidhrama and leaves.*

BODHIDHARMA
Enlightenment can only come in the form of an instantaneous insight! Riddles, Koans, demonstrate the absurdity of truth, they make the mind think outside itself. If a tree falls in the forest and no one is there to hear it, does it make a sound?

MONK TWO
Oh! What is the sound of one hand clapping?

MONK THREE
Oh! What did your face look like before you were born?
Seriously I don't know the answer!

BODHIDHARMA
The point isn't to answer! But to think - why can't they be
answered! Real truth is experiential and cannot be
mediated.

MONK ONE
But --

BODHIDHARMA
Shh. Language...science...even this play is subjective and
can't be trusted! *(To audience)* Sorry. The only truth that
Koans show us are in the lingering question marks where
the answer would be if one existed!

*Bodhidharma helps the worried monks "achieve peace,"
putting them in peaceful meditation positions as a look of
bliss crosses their faces.*

Get rid of the distinctions between you and the rest of the
world and you achieve peace. Become one with objective
reality!

*A peaceful beat. Exhale. Bodhidharma breaks:*

We not only meditate! We move! Strenuous exercises! Go!
Go! Go!

*He bosses them around and makes them work out
together.*

MONK TWO
Oh!

MONK ONE
This is hard work!

MONK THREE
Or as we say in Chinese: Kung Fu!

BODHIDARMA
Oh I like the sound of that.

*Wu pops up and is pissed.*

WU
This is crazy! You've taken over my mountain! I'll take care of you!

*Bodidharma quickly takes care of Wu in Kung Fu movie style.*

WU
Ah!!

*Wu collapses. Monks react in amazement, look to Bodhidharma.*

BODHIDHARMA
I'm also toying with idea of it being a personal defense system.

MONKS
Yay!

*Monk party time!*

MONK ONE
This is the best monk party we've ever had!

*Bodhidharma puts a sandal on top of his head, leaving.*

MONK THREE
Wait! Where are you going?

MONK TWO
And why are you wearing a sandal on top of your head?

*Bodhidharma waits to see. Monk Three learns:*

MONK THREE
There is no answer.

*Bodhidharma smiles for the first time at us. It might still be scary. He exits.*

MONK TWO
Wait for me!

*He puts his sandal on top of his head and follows.*

MONK ONE
Wow. How did you know-

*Monk Three turns, now the master:*

MONK THREE
INSTANTANEOUS INSIGHT!!!

*A light bulb swings down, and lights up! But Descartes runs on holding his jacket over his head trying to hide from the light. He unscrews the light bulb, which goes out. Darkness. Those actors playing Monks blurt out:*

ACTORS
Descartes!

**LADIES & GENTS! THE FATHER OF MODERN PHILOSOPHY ACTION PHILOSOPHER #4! DESCARTES!**

*Frenchy music. Descartes speaks from offstage. Actors remain onstage. Since this is all in "Descartes' world," they can speak in French accents, smoke, light up cigarettes, carry baguettes, etc.*

DESCARTES (OFF)
Bonsoir! It is me again. The French guy. I still have a lit-tle problem...*(Laughs nervously)* If you think about it ... how do you know if we exist or not?

ACTOR ONE
Use your eyes, dumbass. You can see you exist.

DESCARTES (OFF)
But wow, can I trust my senses? They are so easily deceived!

*Projection: The famous face/vase optical illusion drawn in the comic below:*

DESCARTES
See? Does this image depict a vase? Or a pair of faces?

ACTOR TWO
Vase!

ACTOR THREE
Faces!

ACTOR FOUR
Daddy, why are you hurting Mommy? Where are your
clothes? Get off of him, or is that the mailman? I mean
vases, I see that, totally.

DESCARTES (OFF)
Okay, weird guy - the point is how do I know this exchange
is really taking place? For all I know, I could be asleep and
dreaming it!

ACTOR FIVE *(Points to guy in audience)*
Like that guy! Wake up!

DESCARTES (OFF)
Yes, wake him up! Pay attention! I am trying to prove I am
even here, okay? Because God Himself could be a cruel
deceiver, purposefully flooding my senses with
misinformation!

ACTOR THREE
But...doesn't the fact that you doubt your own existence
count for anything?

ACTOR FIVE
Yeah- that mode of thought is real.

ACTOR TWO
So that's gotta emanate from some actual entity!

DESCARTES (OFF)
Sacre bleu! You are right!

*The actors exit. The light bulb lights up again burning brightly! Descartes runs on.*

DESCARTES
I THINK, THEREFORE I AM!

*The French music swells as does Descartes' pride as he continues to prove this.*

My soul holds this idea with such clarity, it must be true. I will use that clarity as a guide as I review the other ideas in my mind to see if they are true as well! My senses suggest that my soul/mind is attached to some kind of body. But can I trust my senses?

*To a woman in the audience.*

I can't mentally make this woman disappear, so it's possible she exists independently from my mind!
I can see her, touch her, smell her ... and since my senses are part of my body and not of my mind, I cannot be creating these wonderful stimuli myself. So! If the idea of this being was placed into my mind from outside of me, the cause must have as much reality as I conceive to be in the beautiful woman itself!

*Actor Four bounds back on.*

ACTOR FOUR
OMG! That's the PRINCIPLE OF SUFFICIENT REASON!

DESCARTES
Oui, and if so, if I have the innate idea of a God that is infinitely perfect...

*Jesus comes back on wearing Mickey Mouse ears from Disneyland. Since he is in Descartes' world now, he has a very Frenchy accent.*

JESUS
Oui! I am back from Disneyland, and I am AWESOME!

DESCARTES
Only fallible, finite me could only have been caused by a perfect, infinite source!  Our innate idea of the infinitely perfect God is the mark of the craftsman stamped on his work!

*Jesus stamps Descartes on his forehead.*

JESUS
C'est Magnifique!

DESCARTES
Merci. If God is perfect, it follows that he is not a deciever! He is <u>not</u> flooding my senses with false information!

JESUS
Why would I do that?

DESCARTES
Because you are awesome and even though I'm standing next to my hero Jesus *(pinches himself)* I know I am not dreaming this, for memory ties the events of our waking lives together. In a dream I do not remember all the dreams I had before that one. I remember all of my life up until this point, so I must be awake. Therefore, I have no other choice than to conclude that I receive perceptions of an external world because an external world actually exists! Yes! Whew! Okay. Now that I've proven that I exist,

DESCARTES (CONT.)
....we exist, are here - I can do my bit, which you are going to love.

*Actor Four gets him his guitar and everyone gathers around like on Mr. Rogers. Actor playing Descartes can feel free to add to his description of the song.*

This song hit me when I was walking through the park and I saw a dead squirrel lying on the ground and suddenly – voila! I knew every answer to every question in the universe, and I put it in this song. I worked on it for many years, and you will love it. Everyone feel free to sing along. In the key of G.

*Starts strumming, singing:*

I was born in –

*Nietzche approaches.*

NIETZSCHE
NEIN! Too late! There is no time for your silly song.

*Actors get upset, and Descartes insists they want to hear the song, but Nietzsche gestures for him to go. Descartes, sad and a bit pissed, does.*

DESCARTES
Jerk.

*Nietzsche looks at Jesus and dramatically proclaims:*

NIETZSCHE
God ... is dead!

*Aw! Jesus drops his cross sadly and drags it away as the end of the Mickey Mouse club song plays. Jesus looks back here and there, in case someone asks him to stay. They don't. They wave goodbye. He goes.*

NIETZSCHE
And if God is dead ...

*Nietzsche takes off his big black glasses a la Clark Kent.*

I remember who I am!

## NEW AND IMPROVED ACTION PHILOSPHER #5: FRIEDRICH NIETZSCHE!

*Superman Theme music plays. A Big Man beats up everyone.*

ANNOUNCER
In a teeming Metropolis, a horrible big man is beating up everyone he can get his big man hands on!

NIETZSCHE: *(as "Clark Kent")*
Hmmm – This looks like a job for..."my other self."

*Transforms into Übermensch, "flies" off.*

CITY PERSON ONE
Look – it's a phenomenologist!

CITY PERSON TWO
Look -- it's Schopenhauer's will to power!

CITY PERSON THREE
No it's a plane!

CITY PERSON ONE
It's the Übermensch! He'll save us!

NIETZSCHE
Ah! Way to go Big Man! Here – you missed this guy.

*Nietzsche beats up City Person One.*

CITY PERSON TWO
But aren't you going to do something, Ubermensch?

NIETZSCHE
Why should I? Equality is a human-created concept bogus and ultimately corrupting...the one true law of the universe is: 99 % of everything is shit!

CITYPERSON ONE
The Übermensch is a dick.

*Big Man poses and shows off his Big Man muscles as Nietzsche admires and seemingly approves.*

NIETZSCHE
Look. When we see a big fish get ready to swallow a little fish, we say: "Ah there's such balance in nature! Only the fittest can survive. It's so beautiful and wise!" But when the big person does more or less the same thing to a little person, we say—

CITY PERSON THREE
You're evil and immoral, not to mention arrogant!

BIG MAN
What big man do? What big man do?

NIETZSCHE
Don't you worry, big man! Keep plugging away! Dominate! See, equality is phony and unnatural because just like fish, some people are bigger, stronger and smarter than others - but they are persecuted for acting like it! Some people act like big fish all the time. This concept of "equality" is corrupting because it makes us hypocrites for following something we know (unconsciously or not) to be a lie.

*Big Man lets out an excited cry or runs around happy.*

BIG MAN
Yes! Am I really super?

NIETZSCHE
You? *(Laughs uproariously)* No, no, no. You're just big.
You're still incredibly stupid, only able to dominate others
through sheer physical strength. That's not right. Or wrong.
It simply is.

*Big Man cries.*

NIETZSCHE
No room for tears here. You may cry outside.

*Big Man wanders off. Nietzsche/Ubermensch faces the
press.*

NIETZSCHE
Ubermensch will take your questions now, Planet Daily
Super Hero Paper!!

REPORTER ONE
How did you get your powers Ubermensch? From falling in
a vat of acid?

REPORTER TWO
Some distant star?

REPORTER THREE
Bitten by a really domineering spider?

NIETZSCHE
NO!  Tens of thousands of years ago, the smartest and
strongest of any given group – THE REAL SUPERMAN –
ME! -- naturally became their ruler. And all the other
cavemen-like losers are like:

*The Reporters turn around, now becoming Cavemen in the Ubermensche's "origin story."*

CAVEMAN ONE
I'm tired of superman getting all that tail!

CAVEMAN TWO
The superman kicked my ass for not working the mammoth pits!

CAVEMAN THREE
We must think of ... duh ... sumpin' to get dat sooperman!

CAVEMAN ONE
Us jealous masses gotta get together and invent something to bring him down!

CAVE MAN TWO
Okay what?

CAVEMAN THREE
Religion!

CAVEMAN TWO
What's that?

*The big cross rises up or is held by other actors as holy music plays. Nietzsche looks around freaked out.*

GOD'S VOICE (OFF STAGE)
I am God! I am an invisible, supernatural entity that is greater than the superman! You must obey me, not him! And because I am invisible, all my commands must be dictated by ... the priest race here.

*The cavemen are confused. Who is heck is the Priest race? God chooses the caveman on stage that she would like to be in charge. The chosen one happily grabs the big cross and goes after Neitzshe, who crumples under the kryptonite effect of the cross.*

NEITZSCHE
Right! And, ever since, western society has retained this basic monotheistic ideal. But the master priest class always makes sure it's more equal than others! Since equality is bogus, this opium of the masses is ultimately unsatisfying. With no superman, the always disappointed masses and the master race are locked in a perpetual but meaningless struggle for temporal power. The invention of god made the superman stop believing in his own existence. And this simple idea of mine is misused by the most base, disgusting acts of man!

*Nietzsche/Ubermench collapses. Cavemen turn back into reporters. Nietzsche jumps back up as if he just told them the story.*

REPORTER ONE
What a scoop! Great origin story, Ubermench!

REPORTER TWO
But how can human misery be relieved?

*Oh boy. The know it all Nietzsche clearly doesn't have the answer, but he tries to cover.*

NIETZSCHE
Yeah, Well, um...ah...oh, yes. So—

*Nietzsche runs off. Reporters grumble as they exit off.*

REPORTER ONE
Worst. Superhero. Ever.

*Old Time-y Filmstrips of 1950's milk advertisements play.*
*Freddy, an actor playing a young kid in a beanie, runs on.*

FREDDY
Mom says –

*Mom enters tossing him a football.*

MOM
Freddy, the whole point of living is to make money!

*She quickly kisses Freddy and goes on her way to work.*

FREDDY
Then why are things like milk so cheap and things like this
fancy football so expensive? Shouldn't things be reversed?
Why does milk cost less than gold?

*Happy 50's educational music plays as Karl Marx*
*magically appears next to Freddy.*

MARX
To answer your question, Freddy, we'll have to take a little
trip!

FREDDY
Oh, boy! KARL MARX!

**YUP, THAT'S RIGHT! WELCOME TO:**
**ACTION PHILOSOPHER #6: KARL MARX!**

MARX
A magical mystery trip...into the wonderful, splendiferous
world...of commodities!

*They twirl around. Projections of commodities may twirl
around them.*

FREDDY
Jinkers! What the hell is a commodity?

MARX
Didn't read your Das Kapital, eh Freddy? Naughty boy! *(he
laughs)* A commodity is an object made outside of us, a
thing that by its properties satisfies human wants. The
nature of such wants, whether they spring from the
stomach or from fancy, makes no difference!

FREDDY
Why?

MARX
The utility of a thing makes it a use value – how it's useful
is irrelevant. It's about consumption. A thing has value
only because of human labor! The magnitude of this value
is measured by the quantity of the labor. Quantity of labor
is measured by duration– time!

*An actor playing a Worker excitedly "milks" a small cut out
cow by pumping its teeny tail faster and faster. When he's
done with his task, his finished product appears – a milk
carton full of milk!*

FREDDY
So...it takes less time to milk a cow than it does to mine gold... and that's why milk's cheaper?

MARX
HA, HA! Now let's not start jumping to conclusions, Freddy!

*A Customer comes to buy the milk. Worker and Customer barter for money over the milk.*

To become a commodity, a product must be transferred to another, by means of an exchange. But a commodity's exchange value always ends up being greater than the labor time invested in it! In Marxian economics, this excess is known as surplus value...or capital!

*Capitalist, wearing a huge black top hat - appears over Worker and Customer! He takes all the money and the carton of milk, drinks greedily, and smiles.*

Capitalists benefit from the exchange, not production of commodities. We call them the bourgeoisie! Middle classes! Factory owners – corporate bigwigs!

FREDDY
Geez...I get it! Workers exchange their labor time for wages...which they give back to the capitalist so they can buy the very commodities they produce! What a vicious cycle! Is there any way it can be broken, Mr. Marx?

*As Marx talks he gets a huge duffel bag.*

MARX
Actually, I can think of 47 ways, Freddy! AKA-47, that is. Let's do this thing.

*Marx stands, transforming into Rambo.*

FREDDY
And … uh … what thing would <u>that</u> be, Mr. Marx?

MARX
I kick ass for the proles!

*Freddy watches in horror as Marx viciously attacks Capitalist.*

FREDDY
B..but, Mr. Marx…maybe…maybe we could talk about this first?

*He finishes, perhaps sawing off/breaking Capitalist's head and tossing the clearly fake head to happy workers.*

MARX
HA, HA! You're so adorably naive Freddy! Seizing the means of production is the only way the workers can end their exploitation for surplus value!

*Sounds of war and explosions erupt around them. They run around fleeing top hat-wearing capitalists who try to take them out.*

FREDDY
Gee wilikers, Mr. Marx…what led to you having such extreme views?

MARX
Gosh knows I didn't start out that way, Freddy! I was born in Prussia in 1818. My dad was a lawyer, and I went to school to study law, but I got bitten by the philosophy bug instead…grenade me, Freddy.

FREDDY
Flashbang or incendiary?

MARX
Incendiary.

*Freddy hands Marx a grenade.*

FREDDY
Here you go.

MARX
Thanks.

*Marx pulls the pin out of the grenade with his teeth, and tosses it over his shoulder. Freddy puts his fingers in his ears.*

MARX
I turned to journalism...worked for a bunch of leftist workers' papers. That got me kicked out of Prussia, France -- wound up in London, where the communist league asked me and Friedrich Engels to write a manifesto on their behalf. That was in 1847. Became a big wheel in the movement after that. Traveled all over Europe, organizing workers' parties. Everywhere I saw the same poverty and MISERY among the workers – the same forced ignorance! Like we wrote – "What the bourgeoisie produces, above all–"

*Marx shoots another capitalist.*

FREDDY
-- is its own grave diggers." Its fall and the victory of the proletariat are equally inevitable. Your manifesto. It's beautiful.

*Marx smiles. Everything is going to hell around them.*

FREDDY (CONT.)
B...but, I mean, the overthrow of all social conditions? Is that really necessary? Y..you know, since you were alive, a lot of positive things have happened in capitalist society – labor unions, socialized medicine, minimum wage, child labor laws...

*Marx turns on Freddy, who cowers and loses it.*

MARX
Band aids on a cancer patient! What does the label on your shirt say, Fred? Made in China.

FREDDY
But don't you think it's unrealistic to think people will stop being competitive and just start sharing with each other? Human nature is obsessed with status–

MARX
"Human nature?"

*Over Freddy's shoulder, Marx shoots a familiar looking woman passing by – Freddy's mom! Freddy doesn't see. She slumps over.*

MARX
Ha, ha! You're too young to believe in fairy tales, you little scamp! *(Tousles his hair)* The material conditions of our lives determine this "human nature" not the other way around! The first step toward Communism...is to get rid of the capitalists!

*Smart, classical music plays. Pompous Professor from Plato's story appears finishing his lecture. As he does, Marx takes Freddy's football and gives Freddy his knife.*

PROFESSOR
... and that's why the classic video game Burger Time holds all the secrets of the universe. Now students, be sure to sign up for my class next semester: classic Marxist power constructions in film noir at NYU!

*Freddy suddenly jumps on Professor, stabbing him. Even Marx is taken aback.*

FREDDY
DIE, TOOL OF THE OPPRESSORS! DIE!!

PROFESSOR
NO! Gak...Ugh!

FREDDY
I don't know what came over me...that guy was just...too annoying to live!

MARX
That's my boy! "If that is Marxism, I am not a Marxist!" Intellectuals – writers – may serve a movement as its mouthpiece but cannot create it. Only the masses can liberate the masses!

*As Marx talks, he props up the Professor's struggling body, takes out a pair of pliers, and starts to pry something out of the Professor's mouth.*

FREDDY
But you never did answer my question...

MARX
What the hell is that again?

FREDDY
Why is Gold more expensive than milk?

*Happy 50's music comes back on.*

MARX
Oh! Well, to maximize capital, workers are paid as little as possible. Capitalists need to keep them alive to pump out more laborers, so necessities of life must remain cheap and plentiful so workers can buy them even with their wages– and that's why milk is cheaper than gold!

*Marx finally holds up what he pried from the now silent Professor: a gold tooth.*

What do you think Freddy?

FREDDY
I want my Mommy!

*Uh-oh. Marx looks at woman's body still lying there– Freddy's mom's body. He tries to hide her, but Freddy now sees.*

MARX
Ooh. Sorry. You didn't tell me she worked in a bank. I can't help it! It's instinct when I see the bourgeoisie! Freddy. C'mon.

*Freddy runs off crying.*

We still have to take care of all these capitalist pigs!

*He starts to go after the audience with his gun, raising it up when Rand enters with her books as weapons to face him.*

RAND
Give it up Marx! The only moral political system is laissez-faire capitalism!

*Marx shoots, but she uses her books like Wonder Woman bracelets and deflects them.*

Hah! No one can get through *Atlas Shrugged*.

*Plato comes on with a chair as his weapon.*

PLATO
Plato so not getting into politics– they always throw me in jail.

RAND
But you're revered. You know who follows me? Allan Greenspan!

*Descartes comes back on waving the huge cross in front of him to protect himself.*

DESCARTES
Hey! You didn't have your dead body torn apart by overzealous zealots!

MARX
They call Obama a Marxist! Obama! Did you see his bailout of the auto industry?

*Bodhidharma creeps on, gets close to Marx with a sandal in his hand, seemly being peaceful.*

**BODHIDHARMA**
Enter the silence! Become ONE with objective REALITY.

*Bodhidharma gleefully smacks Marx in the head with his sandal.*

**RAND**
He is annoying! And no one ever understands any of our ideas!

**PLATO**
But all we have is our philosophy!

*They all start arguing - shouting lines from their philosophy at each other – many of which we've heard earlier. They grow louder and louder until another voice overrides them.*

**SARTRE**
Non.

*Lights go out! Darkness. Someone whispers, "Sartre!" And sure enough, a figure is seen, lighting up a cigarette. Café music is heard. Spotlight on Sartre against the wall with the microphone.*

**SARTRE**
In the face of death, only man can make himself. Only he, using his intentional consciousness can choose acts that lead him to his ideal self! That means mankind is condemned to be free.

**PLATO**
But existence emanates from a higher essence!

SARTRE
Non! Existence precedes essence!

DESCARTES
I think therefore I --

SARTRE
Non! No one just thinks. One always thinks about something. The only accurate way to evaluate consciousness is through "pure subjectivity." I have an appointment with my friend at 4 o'clock. I arrive at the café a quarter of an hour late. My friend is always punctual. Will he have waited for me? When I enter this café to search for him, there is formed a synthetic organization of all the objects in the café as the ground on which my friend is given as about to appear. I am witness to the successive disappearance of all the objects which I look at -- in particular of the faces which detain me for an instant - could any of you be my friend?

*Descartes starts to go to him, but Sartre turns away from him.*

So a café is never "objectively" just a café! In this instance, it has been constructed by my consciousness, Sartre's consciousness as the space where he could be.

*To Descartes:*

Your error was to think of consciousness as somehow transcendent from reality, looking down on it. But really, you exist within the world and it is only through your consciousness that you can make any sense of the world at all.

DESCARTES
I think - I see what you mean!

RAND
Oh like we're going to listen to a socialist.

MARX
My idea of materialistic determinism can't fit into this "man is condemned to be free" business...!

SARTRE
Our ideas exist. But us? Nothing is or can be definite.

RAND
So this can't be happening.

PLATO
But we're here.

RAND
No.

BODHIDHARMA
Maybe?

MARX
We exist. To not exist?

SARTRE
It's true. Hell is other philosophers.

*Sartre goes. They all walk away, heads down depressed, except for Descartes. He looks up at the light bulb which is sadly off.*

DESCARTES
Am I really here?

*He tests it – tries to command light bulb.*

I think therefore I am!

*The light bulb lights up. He smiles, proud.*

Ah! Some ideas do stay. Now I will do my song!

*Everyone reenters, excited. Someone hands him the guitar.*

Oh you will love it! It will tell you everything you ever wanted to know about this life, death and beyond the stars, and it might also be about a whale I once saw. But it will tell you – yes – all the secrets of the universe, make you forever - happy.  Ready?

*He raises his hand to start strumming. The light bulb above him goes out, followed quickly by all the lights. In darkness:*

Merde!

*Lights come up and everyone takes an action packed bow!*

BLACKOUT.

**END OF PLAY.**

**CRYSTAL SKILLMAN** is an award winning Brooklyn based playwright. She is the author of GEEK!, and CUT, both Critics' Picks from the *NY Times*, and WILD which debuted in Chicago, followed by New York earning three New York Innovation Award nominations. Her first produced full length play THE VIGIL or THE GUIDED CRADLE won the 2010 New York Innovative Theatre Award for Outstanding Full-Length Script. New plays include ANOTHER KIND OF LOVE, KING KIRBY, co-written with her wonderful hubby Fred Van Lente of course, and DRUNK ART LOVE. She is working on the books of two musicals with composer Bobby Cronin (CONCRETE JUNGLE, MARY & MAX). In addition to Chicago Dramaworks, Crystal's work is published by Samuel French, featured in several Smith & Kraus as well as Applause books, including *The Best American Short Plays*, and available on **indietheaternow.com**. Crystal is represented by Amy Wagner and Ron Gwiazda at Abrams Artists Agency in NY, and James Beresford with Shepard Management in the UK. She loves theater and comics and philosophy!

**FRED VAN LENTE** is the Harvey Award-nominated and *New York Times* best-selling author of *Incredible Hercules* (with Greg Pak) and *Marvel Zombies 3*, as well as the American Library Association Award–winning *Action Philosophers*. His other comics include *The Comic Book History of Comics*, *The Complete Silencers*, *Brain Boy*, *Archer & Armstrong*, *MODOK's 11*, *X-Men Noir*, *Conan the Avenger*, and *Amazing Spider-Man*. *Wizard* magazine nominated Van Lente for 2008 Breakout Talent (Writer). Comic Book Resources' *Comics Should Be Good* blog named him "one of the 365 Reasons to Love Comics." He's been called *"one of the most idiosyncratic and insightful new voices in comics."* Learn more about him than you can possibly stand at his official website, FredVanLente.com.

**RYAN DUNLAVEY** is a New York City–based artist whose comic work includes *The Comic Book History of Comics*, *Dirt Candy*, *MODOK: Reign Delay*, *Li'l Classix*, *G.I. Joe*, *Tommy Atomic*, and the Xeric and American Library Association Award–winning *Action Philosophers*. His artwork has appeared in *Mad*, *Wizard*, *ToyFare*, *Disney Adventures*, and *Royal Flush*. In 2009, a retrospective of his work was exhibited at the Museum of Comic and Cartoon Art (MoCCA) in New York City. He is wanted for war crimes in seventeen countries. RyanDArtist.com

*Action Philosophers* started off as a one-off Nietzsche gag strip (you know, as you do), that became a self-publishing comics phenomenon that told the lives and thoughts of history's A-list brain trust in a hip and humorous comic book fashion across nine issues, four paperback books and one tenth anniversary hardcover that came out from Dark Horse Comics in 2014, winning a Xeric Award, an American Library Association Great Graphic Novel for Teens Award, an Ignatz Award nomination, and a play. The play that you're reading now, dummy.

### *Action Philosophers: The Theme Song!*

Lyrics and Music by Neimah Djourabchi and Joe Mathers

"WHEN LIFE IS MEANINGLESS WHO DO YOU TURN TO?"

ACTION PHILOSOPHERS *(ACTION! ACTION!)*
THE SMARTEST AND STRONGEST AROUND!
ACTION PHILOSOPHERS *(ACTION! ACTION!)*
THEY'LL KICK YOUR DUMB ASS TO THE GROUND!

PLATO AND BODHI,
AYN RAND AND KARL MARX,
NIETZSCHE AND SARTRE,
AND DON'T FORGET DESCARTES!

ACTION PHILOSOPHERS *(ACTION! ACTION!)*
WITH YOU IN YOUR DARKEST HOUR!
ACTION PHILOSOPHERS *(ACTION! ACTION!)*
EACH HAS THEIR OWN SEPARATE POWERS!

PLATO WILL SMASH YOU,
BODHI DOES KUNG FU,
AYN RAND'S A TOUGH CHICK,
NIETZSCHE A BIG DICK,
PRETTY BOY DESCARTES SMOKES CIGARETTES WITH SARTRE,
YOU'RE GONNA LOVE IT WHEN KARL MARX BLOWS UP SHIT

THEY'RE SO COOL!

ACTION PHILOSOPHERS *(ACTION! ACTION!)*
DON'T GIVE A FUCK WHAT YOUR PARENTS SAY (FUCK EM)!
ACTION PHILOSOPHERS *(ACTION! ACTION!)*
GO OUT AND BUY THEM TODAY!

*All accessories are choking hazards.*

## ALSO AVAILABLE FROM CHICAGO DRAMAWORKS

**THE BEAR SUIT OF HAPPINESS by Evan Linder.** In 1943, Woody, a young gay American, enlists in the army. After being shipped out to a remote Pacific Island, he is given an order: "Put up a show to entertain the men. Keep it simple. Needs music. And they like drag." Theatre of war and theatre of the mind play out together on Woody's little stage as he battles to build an identity and to be free. "This is a piece that stays with you." Chris Jones, *Chicago Tribune.* [4M]

**BODIES AT REST & Other One Act Plays by Eric Peter Schwartz.** Ranging from the funny to the tragic, the three original plays in this collection have two themes in common – morality and strangers. Features *Bodies at Rest, His Last Gun,* and *Pater Angelus.*

**CHORDS by Patricia Kane.** In this one-act play, two middle-aged sisters from Tennessee reunite to record a Christmas record for their eighty year-old grandfather who raised them. Funny and touching, yet unsentimental, CHORDS explores what keeps us fighting for family when that's all it seems we have in common. [3W, 1M]

**UNSHELVED by Beth Kander.** *On what - or whom - does your own identity depend?* The Hollingsworth family is, at first glance, perfectly normal – maybe a bit more literature-centric and a bit more formal than average, but nothing revolutionary. Audrey is the head librarian at the local library, her husband Bill is an English professor, and their son Rye is trying to make it as a writer. When Audrey is diagnosed with early-onset Alzheimer's disease, the calm family picture begins to blur. Before her illness, Audrey had always protected her son and husband; now, as she sinks into the past, she reveals long-buried family secrets. [2M, 2F]

**Find scripts and licensing information for all plays at
www.ChicagoDramaworks.com**

CPSIA information can be obtained
at www.ICGtesting.com
Printed in the USA
LVOW01s1217140317
527168LV00006B/903/P